Public Lending Right

Annual Report and
Account 2004 - 2005

Ordered by the House of Commons to be printed 18 July 2005

Report, by the Secretary of State for Culture, Media and Sport, on the PLR Scheme 2004-05,
incorporating the Registrar's Annual Review, presented to Parliament pursuant to Section 3(8) of the
Public Lending Right Act 1979; Account, of the Public Lending Right Central Fund, presented to
Parliament pursuant to Section 2(6) of the PLR Act 1979, for the year ended 31 March 2005.

HC 199   LONDON: The Stationery Office   £16.60

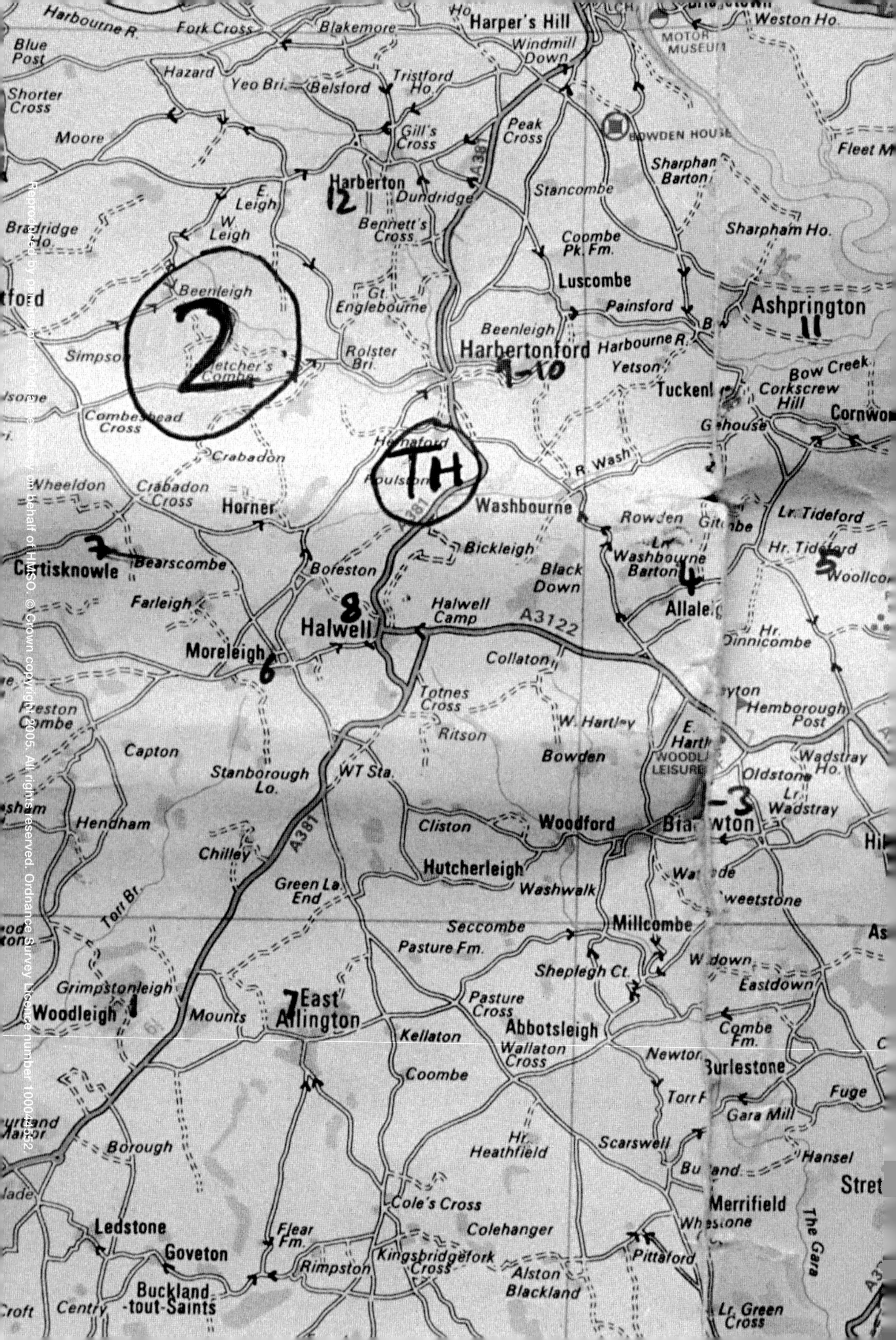
Harbourne R.
Fork Cross
Blakemore
Harper's Hill
Weston Ho.
Motor Museum
Blue Post
Windmill Down
Hazard
Yeo Bri.
Belsford
Tristford Ho.
Shorter Cross
Peak Cross
Bowden House
Moore
Gill's Cross
Fleet Mill
A381
Sharpham Barton
Harberton
12
Dundridge
Stancombe
E. Leigh
W. Leigh
Bradridge Ho.
Bennett's Cross
Sharpham Ho.
Coombe Pk. Fm.
Beenleigh
Luscombe
2
Gt. Englebourne
Painsford
Ashprington
11
Simpson
Fletcher's Combe
Rolster Bri.
Beenleigh
Harbertonford
Harbourne R.
1-10
Yetson
Bow Creek
Corkscrew Hill
Combeshead Cross
Cornworthy
Crabadon
TH
R. Wash
Wheeldon
Crabadon Cross
Horner
Washbourne
Rowden
Lr. Tideford
Bickleigh
Lr. Washbourne Barton
Hr. Tideford
3
Bearscombe
Boreston
Black Down
4
5
Farleigh
8
Halwell Camp
Allaleigh
Halwell
A3122
Hr. Dinnicombe
Moreleigh
6
Collaton
Totnes Cross
Hemborough Post
Preston Combe
W. Hartley
Ritson
Capton
Bowden
Wadstray Ho.
Stanborough Lo.
WT Sta.
Oldstone
Lr. Wadstray
-3
Hendham
Cliston
Woodford
Chilley
A381
Hutcherleigh
Washwalk
Green La. End
Torr Br.
Seccombe
Millcombe
Pasture Fm.
Shepleigh Ct.
Eastdown
Grimpstonleigh
7 East Allington
Pasture Cross
Woodleigh
Mounts
Abbotsleigh
Combe Fm.
Kellaton
Wallaton Cross
Burlestone
Coombe
Fuge
Gara Mill
Hr. Heathfield
Scarswell
Borough
Hansel
Cole's Cross
Merrifield
Ledstone
Flear Fm.
Colehanger
The Gara
Goveton
Kingsbridgefork Cross
Pittaford
Rimpston
Alston
Buckland-tout-Saints
Blackland
Centry
Lr. Green Cross

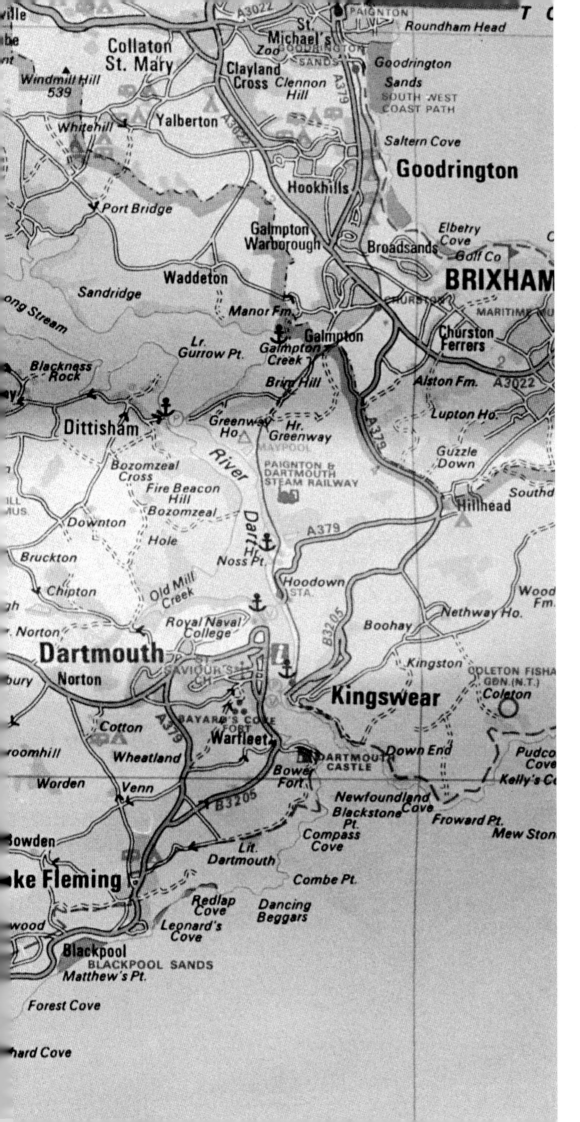

PLR is very grateful to Devon Library and Information Services for making possible the illustrations for this year's Report. These photographs document a day in the life of a mobile library, it's users and librarian Steve Palmer as he makes books and other media accessible to borrowers round the Blackawton to Harberton route south of Totnes. We also wish to acknowledge the generosity of all those who appear in these photographs. Devon is a PLR sample authority.

Report on the
**Public Lending Right
Scheme** and Account
2004-2005

The cover shows the Devon Library and Information Services mobile library, on the Blackawton to Harberton route. The frontispiece pictures are of Steve Palmer, the librarian, followed by a map of the route. The title pages show Tom Jaine and 'Cherie' in Allaleigh. The section heads show a detail from the cab *(The Registrar's Annual Review)*, Colin Revell in Curtisknowle *(Scheme Developments)* and route *(Guest Features)*. The end page is from the Jeffery family's weekend break in Cornwall.

Design and art direction by Antman
Photography by Steve Benbow
Scanning by Peninsular Services
Printing and finishing by Maslands

Contents

Preface

I have pleasure in laying before Parliament this Report on the operation of the Public Lending Right Scheme for 2004-05.

PLR plays a vital role in supporting the country's authors. The Scheme makes an important contribution to my Department's wider aims for the creative economy. This year over 18,000 writers, illustrators, editors and translators received a payment reflecting the use made by the public of their books in libraries. Payments are made on the basis of a rate per loan. This year's rate, at 5.26 pence, is the highest to date.

As can be seen from the Registrar's annual review, he and his team have been busy during the year, taking forward a number of projects aimed at improving the service they provide to authors and libraries. I have been particularly impressed by the enthusiastic take-up of the new on-line services by authors, and this says much for the care taken by the PLR team in designing a user-friendly system. Much progress has also been made in providing the library community with on-line access to PLR's unique database of data on book borrowing trends across the country's public libraries. I commend the Registrar's initiative in this area. The information is already being used by partner organisations such as The Reading Agency to support reader development initiatives in libraries that clearly indicates the potential of this new data source.

The Department is working in partnership with the Registrar and the Advisory Committee in seeing some changes to the Scheme through Parliament. These changes are aimed at supporting PLR's plans to modernise the Scheme and make it more responsive to authors' needs. I am pleased to have secured an increase in PLR's fund to £7.6m from 2006-07 flowing from the latest Spending Review.

I am grateful to Jim Parker and his team at the PLR office for all their hard work in managing PLR so successfully, and my thanks also go to Simon Brett and the members of the PLR Advisory Committee for their advice on the Scheme's operation. The recognition of PLR's importance for authors provided by the recent House of Commons Culture, Media and Sport Select Committee Report on Public Libraries is ample testimony to the success of the PLR team's management of the Scheme.

The Rt Hon Tessa Jowell MP
Secretary of State for Culture, Media and Sport

An Interview with Dr Jim Parker, Registrar
Overview: A Year at Public Lending Right

Jim Parker has been Registrar of Public Lending Right since 1991. During the past fourteen years he has overseen considerable changes both to the Scheme and the management and operational aspects of its operation. The public library sample has increased from 2% to 20% of book loans nationally; registered authors and other rights-holders have increased by 75%, and government funding has grown by 40%. This, together with the application of enhanced technology, has improved PLR's efficiency and effectiveness, reducing the operational costs to 11% of turnover.

The total fund for 2004-05 was £7.38 million ensuring the highest rate per loan for rights-holders to date at 5.26 pence. Since 1979, PLR has distributed over £89 million to the nation's authors.

Knowing that PLR never rests on its laurels in its commitment to its rights-holders, what have been the most significant steps forward this year?

JP: There's been considerable progress with the Scheme's modernisation this year. We've developed initiatives such as on-line registration, which has proved very popular with authors, and increased automation of loans data collection systems, that allows us to keep costs down while enabling us to bring more library authorities into the sample. We have continued to build public awareness of what we do, and how important it is for authors, through our increasingly successful media campaigns.

As the 25th Anniversary celebrations drew to a close at the end of the year, what legacy has this given PLR to take forward?

JP: The 25th Anniversary celebrations brought home to us just how

14

many organisations there are who could benefit from the work we do for authors. We now recognise how useful our extensive database of information on book borrowing trends will be to a wide range of partners.

The LEWIS facility, with its unique ability to apply the book trade's standard subject categories to book loans data, has been warmly welcomed by librarians as a breakthrough.

JP: We have taken great strides in providing new and sophisticated access routes into this database. The LEWIS facility will provide on-line access for the library community to PLR's loans database; its unique ability to apply the book trade's standard subject categories to book loans data has been warmly welcomed by librarians as a breakthrough. We are very conscious of our membership of the DCMS family and the opportunities this offers to support wider initiatives in our sector. We were delighted to make our loans data available to support the groundbreaking reader development work undertaken by The Reading Agency.

PLR has been described as a role model for Schemes around the globe. What have recent collaborations abroad led to?

JP: After what had seemed like years of inaction following the passing of the European Community's lending right directive in 1992, we're now seeing a flurry of activity. PLR systems have sprung up in the new East European member states, and the European Commission has

The Story of Public Lending Right
1946 - 2004

1946	First PLR system set-up – in Denmark
1950	Catherine Cookson's first book, Kate Hannigan
1951	Author John Brophy proposes a lending right for British authors
1966	Last of Boots subscription libraries closes
1972	Maureen Duffy & Brigid Brophy set up Writers Action Group to fight for PLR
1979	Labour Government passes Public Lending Right Act
1981	Appointment of John Sumsion as first PLR Registrar
1982	PLR Scheme gets parliamentary approval
	First Waterstone's bookshop opened
1984	First payments made to authors with funding of £2 million
1988	PLR Fund increased to £3.5 million
1989	PLR's library sample grows from 20 to 30 library authorities
1992	EU Lending Right Directive passed
1993	Department of National Heritage (now DCMS) created
1997	Net Book Agreement ruled illegal
1999	Arts Minister Alan Howarth opens new PLR offices
2000	PLR extended to all European Union authors
	150th anniversary of 1850 Public Libraries Act
2001	Authors campaign for increased PLR funding
2003	Jacqueline Wilson succeeds Catherine Cookson as the UK's top lending author
2002	PLR Fund up to £7 million. Rate Per Loan now 4.21 pence
2004	PLR celebrates its 25th anniversary

threatened some of the more established states with legal action if they don't implement the Directive properly. The programme of PLR seminars that we support has provided a focus for this new interest in PLR and a source of practical assistance for the emerging PLR nations.

And, as you draw a line under the current year, what are the major challenges that lie ahead?

JP: The big issues we face include meeting the Government's targets for efficiency savings, always difficult for small bodies like PLR whose major costs are fixed. We also have to introduce the new 13 digit ISBN which impacts on every part of the PLR operation. There are proposed scheme changes to our payment thresholds awaiting confirmation from DCMS Ministers. We hope to introduce the new thresholds (£6,600 maximum, and £1 minimum) from 2006-07. We're also looking to build on our cultural diversity survey. Our aim is to ensure that authors from every ethnic background know about PLR and are in a position to register with us.

Our aim is to ensure that authors from every ethnic background know about PLR and are in a position to register with us.

The Registrar's Team
The Registrar is supported by Sue Ridge, his PA. Evelyn Relph, Assistant Registrar, is responsible to the Registrar for the day-today running of the PLR; Julia Coxon, E-Business and Project Co-ordinator, reports to the Assistant Registrar.

Table 1
Two Year Comparison
2003/04 - 2004/05

Payment Date	**21st year** Feb 2004	**22nd year** Feb 2005
Expenditure		
Government Funding	£7,200,000	£7,381,000
Operating Costs	£812,000	£812,000
Payments to Authors (to nearest 10,000)	£6,400,000	£6,540,000
Rate Per Loan	4.85p	5.26p
Authors' Earnings		
£6,000	274	285
£5,000 - £6,000	81	70
£2,500 - £4,999.99	350	376
£1,000 - £2,499.99	767	783
£500 - £999.99	910	911
£100 - £499.99	3,875	3,826
£5 - £99.99	12,526	12,415
Total Recipients	18,783	18,666
Registrations		
Total Book 'Interests' (to date)	366,427	383,042
'Interests' Registered to 'New' Authors	4,631	3,755
'Interests' Registered to 'Old' Authors	11,940	12,327
Sample Book Loans		
Total UK Loans	377m	361m
Loans Sampled by PLR	71m	71m
(As % of UK Loans)	19%	20%
Registered Loans (estimated)	169m	158m
(As % of UK Loans)	45%	44%

PLR's full audited accounts
These are prepared on an accruals basis
[see pp 87 to 109]. The summary figures above are
expressed in cash terms and rounded off.

Author and Book Registration

Objective 1
All new authors and
books were registered
by 30 June 2004,
including 1,235
authors registering for
the first time.

Led by Carolyn Gray, the Author Services Team have handled in excess of 120,000 transactions this year. Their job is to ensure that the 35,000 or so registered authors' records are accurately maintained along with the ISBNs for each edition of their work. They also look after the authors, dealing with any queries or worries they may have throughout the year.

A major challenge for the team is the book industry's move from 10-digit to 13-digit ISBNs by the beginning of 2007. In 2005-06 the team will be closely involved in a project to prepare for the change-over.

Objective 2
We aimed to achieve a
95% satisfaction rate
from authors consulted
on the service
provided by PLR.
(100% achieved).

In support of the Government's policies on cultural diversity, PLR has begun an analysis of the ethnicity of its authors. PLR's aim is to ensure that the cultural diversity of UK writers is fully represented amongst registered authors.

A core purpose for PLR is to administer the scheme to the benefit of authors and other rights-holders. The Author Services team are committed to providing the highest quality of service possible and to carrying out regular surveys of authors' views.

Overall we achieved 100% satisfaction with 64% of respondents describing the service as 'excellent'

Registration Specialist, Joanne Gayford, comments on PLR's recent author satisfaction survey
" Between 1 April 2004 and 31 March 2005 we carried out a survey, selecting at random new and existing registered authors. The 51.8% response gave us a great deal of positive feedback as well as some

suggestions for improvement. Overall we achieved 100% satisfaction with 64% of respondents describing the service as 'excellent'." (See survey results overleaf.)

What the Authors said
"I think you do a brilliant job – and it really feels as if you're on the authors' side, so thank you!"
"As a foreigner, and having already applied for PLR in other countries, I can only say that I am most impressed by the speed, accuracy and friendliness [on the phone] of the British PLR staff. Congratulations!"

"As a foreigner, and having already applied for PLR in other countries, I can only say that I am most impressed by the speed, accuracy and friendliness [on the phone] of the British PLR staff. Congratulations!"

Pointers for Improvement
"Being able to check loans-to-date online, although I don't know how practical this would be to administrate."
"E-mail updates may be useful in the future."

Joanne continues, " Speed of service was clearly an issue. With the recruitment of a new part-time Registration Officer our turnaround times are set to improve in the coming year. Some authors requested email access to their loans data, and email updates throughout the year. We let them know that we're developing a password-protected on-line service to allow them access to their PLR 'accounts'."

Objective 3
Undertake survey of ethnic backgrounds of authors registering for PLR. (Survey of 2004-2005 registrations completed and results to be analysed and acted upon during 2005-2006).

Author Feedback
2003/04 - 2004/5

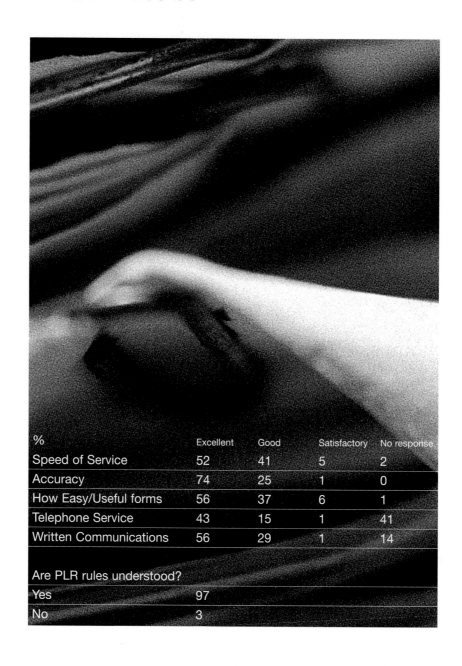

%	Excellent	Good	Satisfactory	No response
Speed of Service	52	41	5	2
Accuracy	74	25	1	0
How Easy/Useful forms	56	37	6	1
Telephone Service	43	15	1	41
Written Communications	56	29	1	14

Are PLR rules understood?	
Yes	97
No	3

E-Registration

The on-line service was launched 18 months ago since when 3,115 users have been enabled. Approximately 40% of book registrations are now submitted on-line. As noted above by Joanne Gayford, the recent author survey showed an overwhelming demand for the facility to view registered books and statements. Work on the second phase of this project will start later in 2005.

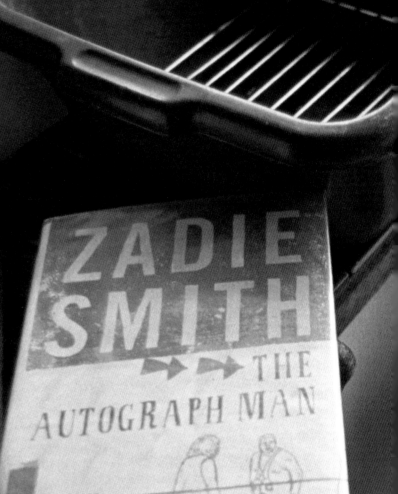

Wendy Harrison: The Autograph Man by Zadie Smith

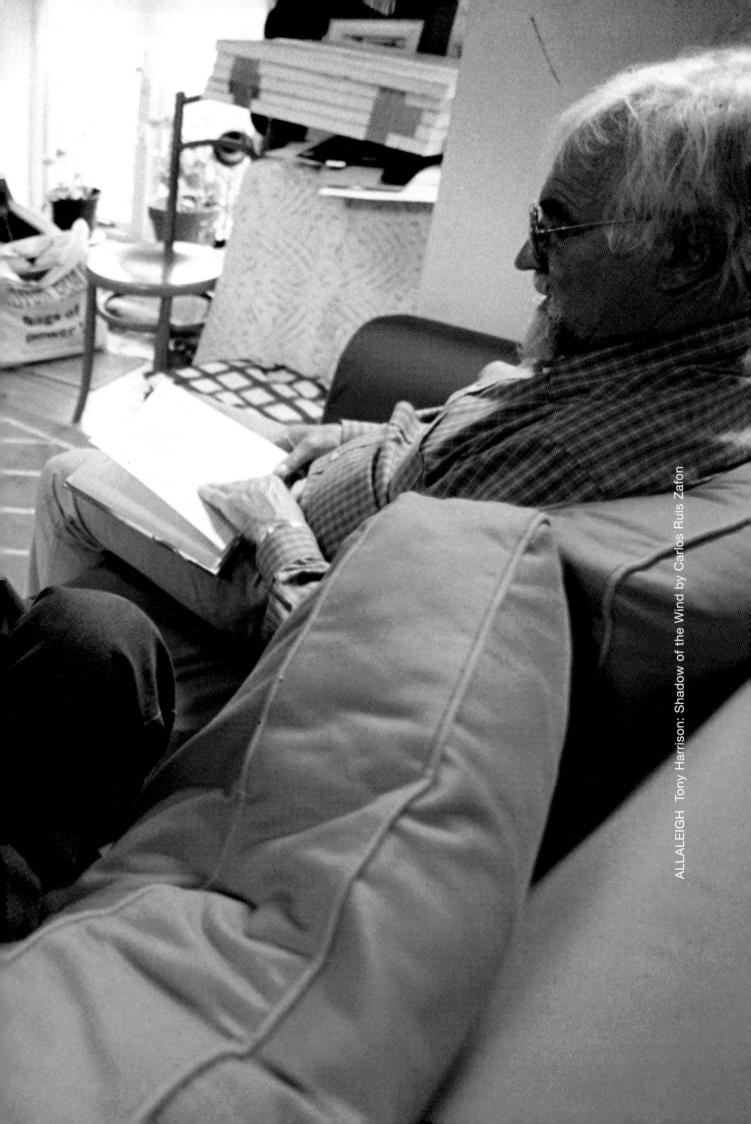

ALLALEIGH Tony Harrison: Shadow of the Wind by Carlos Ruis Zafon

Loans Data Collection

Objective 4
All loans data from the July 2003 – June 2004 library sample was received and processed on target; as planned, we introduced nine new authorities and increased the sample size to 38 authorities for the July 2004 – June 2005 PLR year.

Public Lending Right works closely with the nation's public libraries. They are vital partners in collecting the loans data that is used to estimate the national loans figure for every book registered by authors for PLR.

Loans data comes in throughout the year from library authorities designated by PLR. The Registrar is committed to improving the fairness and representativeness of the sample by increasing its size and range. In July 2004 nine new authorities joined the Scheme; the sample increased to 1,000 service points in 38 authorities; data provided now comprises 20% of all book loans, including 100% coverage of Northern Ireland's libraries. In July 2005 the sample will increase to 39 public library authorities.

Objective 5
We aimed to achieve a satisfaction rate of 95% from sample library authorities consulted on the service provided by PLR. (98% achieved).

The 2004 – 05 reporting year covers two periods of data collection: July 03 – June 04 and July 04 – June 05.

The team leader, Carolyn Gray, reports on the year's key issues
" Every year we carry out a survey of the participating library authorities. We're always looking to improve our service. The survey showed a 98% satisfaction rate against our target of 95% which was hugely encouraging for the team."

" The main request was for access to our data. This will be addressed through the LEWIS project which aims to give all public libraries on-line access to data for stock management purposes within the next two years.

" The major challenge this year has been the switch from UK Marc to Mark 21, in line with the American and Canadian machine readable coding system for books. The British Library decided to adopt this system early in the year. It took us a couple of months to make the transition but it's now safely up and running."

The Team

The Author Services Team is responsible for all services to authors and to libraries in the PLR sample.

The team is led by Carolyn Gray, Author Services Manager. For Services to Authors she is supported by Joanne Gayford, Registration Specialist; Janice Forbes, European Specialist; Kelly Bowstead and Claire Balmer, Registration Officers.

The Services to Libraries unit comprises Sarah Beamson, Library Specialist; and Paul Atkinson, Libraries Officer.

Table 2
Sample Library Authorities
2003/04 and 2004/05

England

Bedfordshire/Luton	Kent	Lancashire
Buckinghamshire/Milton Keynes	Northamptonshire*	Stoke-on-Trent
Devon	Northumberland	Durham*
Somerset*	Hertfordshire*	Southampton*

Metropolitan Districts

Coventry	Stockport*	Leeds
The Wirral	North Tyneside	

Greater London Boroughs

Brent	Kingston upon Thames	Bexley
Harrow		

Wales

Cardiff*	Pembrokeshire	Carmarthenshire
Conwy		

Scotland

Dundee	South Lanarkshire	Fife
Orkney		

Northern Ireland

All five library and education boards are now included in the PLR sample.

* Authorities marked with * were replaced
  in 2004-05 by Bolton, Derby,
  Derbyshire, Hampshire, Nottingham,
  Nottinghamshire, West Sussex,
  Windsor and Maidenhead, and
  Worcestershire.

Payment Distribution

Payment distribution is the climax of a hectic year at PLR. This is the moment when the dedicated work of the Author and Corporate Services Teams bears fruit. All book registrations and sample loans data have been accurately recorded, collated and processed, and finally the rate per loan for payment to authors can be calculated.

Lynn Smith, Business Support Officer, on ensuring that every payment reaches the right author's bank account
" When the distribution finally goes it gives all of us a real sense of satisfaction. There's a whole year's work that goes into getting to that stage – checking, collating, referencing, endless electronic transactions – so much detail that has to be accurate for the system to work and the authors to receive their money.

" When I sit at home with my latest library book I can't help but feel glad that the author is rewarded for the sheer enjoyment I get from reading their work."

61% of the UK's authors earn less than half the national average wage.* But for many it's not just about the money; it's the knowledge that their books are read and enjoyed far beyond the first year of publication.

What Writers Have to Say
" I have good and bad years, but my income is never high and it is no exaggeration to say that I completely rely on my PLR payment." [PLR Authors' Survey].
" It's great to know that people use libraries and borrow my books. PLR is the only true way to tell popularity." [PLR Authors' Survey].

Information about authors' earnings from; Society of Authors Survey of Authors' Earnings: Kate Pool – 'Love Not Money' – 2001. The national average wage: £20,919. 61% of UK authors earn under £10,000.

TIDEFORD CORNER Jill Tregear: Lilies of the Field by Maureen O'Donoghue

Administration

Objective 6
We met our target of containing the Scheme's running costs within our target figure of £812,000; £6.5 million was distributed to authors in payments.

PLR is among the smallest of the bodies that receive their funding from the Department for Culture, Media and Sport. But the Registrar and his team remain aware of the need for robust systems of control in their management of the public money entrusted to them for the Scheme's operation. Accountability systems in place include PLR's three-year Funding Agreement with DCMS setting out key objectives to be achieved in the context of the Department's wider aims for the cultural sector; and external and internal audit provision, monitored by PLR's Audit Committee. The internal auditors concluded that PLR had ' adequate and effective' system controls in place. Key themes this year have been updating PLR's risk management approach and putting in place systems to meet the Registrar's Freedom of Information Act obligations.

Human Resources and Finance

At PLR, unusually, Human Resources and Finance are the responsibility of a single team, led by Janine Armstrong. The team also has responsibility for the distribution of PLR payments. Given the range of new initiatives in the HR and Finance sectors faced by public bodies, it has been a particularly challenging year for the team. Achievements have included:

- met key target (PLR Objective 5) on Scheme's running costs
- gained Investor in People re-accreditation
- commissioned an equal-pay audit of management team salaries
- laid groundwork for new Government HR and pension arrangements
- produced Efficiency Delivery Plan to meet DCMS requirements on future running costs
- managed PLR's Training and Development Plan to ensure PLR has the skills in place to meet its objectives
- managed PLR's Green Strategy, including recycling of 200 bags of paper

- supported development of new automated system (PENNY) for recording 'on-hold' author payments

The Team

The Team is responsible for Human Resources and Finance.

The Team is led by Janine Armstrong, HR & Finance Manager. She is supported by Lynn Smith, Business Support Officer; Kelly Longstaff, Business Support Assistant [appointed May 2005]; and Val Greenan, Administration Officer.

Information Technology

PLR's strategic use of IT underpins everything that it does and helps maintain operating costs at a minimum, ensuring that authors receive the maximum funds.

Among several IT initiatives, this year has seen the development of LEWIS – PLR's Library Enquiry Web Information Service. PLR holds a unique and growing body of data that records book borrowing trends across public libraries. LEWIS is a newly-developed service that can interrogate this data across hundreds of subject categories, and can report on the country's borrowing habits nationally and locally, by particular author, publisher, title, and combinations of these. This information helps to build a fascinating picture of the nation's interests: which cookery books are being borrowed in London compared with Wales; which holiday destination do Northerners prefer; which aspects of our health are we most interested in if we live in the South compared with the North.

Darren Scrafton, PLR's IT Manager on the development of LEWIS

" LEWIS, and its potential for use by the nation's public libraries, is a

Objective 7
Develop LEWIS service to provide library community with enhanced access to PLR's loans database. (Phase 1 complete and LEWIS now available for in-house use).

valuable by-product of an improvement to an internal data management process. We were dealing with an increasing number of requests for information that involved time-consuming trawls through lots of loans data and subsequently we were generating huge reports."

" It was clear that if we could change the approach of requesting the data, to be more specific it would be much more cost and time-effective. We adopted a data-warehouse approach and incorporated the BIC (Book Industry Communications) categories enabling us to identify every genre or type of most of the books listed.

" Realising that this data might be of interest to public libraries the Registrar set up the public library focus group to explore the concept with the profession, and how best to make this data available.

" It was great to be met with so much enthusiasm for the idea at a recent meeting of the group. It gave us a great sense of satisfaction that our attempt to solve an internal problem could help so many more organisations across the UK."

Other IT projects 2004/5

DORIS

PLR's introduction of electronic document systems. Phase 1, electronic copying of all documents leaving the office is now complete. Phase 2, taking electronic copies of all incoming documents, will be completed in 2005/06.

PENNY

The PLR Act requires the Registrar to hold any unclaimed and undistributed payments for up to six years. The specially designed PENNY software system replaces written schedules, streamlining the

Objective 8
Automate in-house financial system which records 'on-hold' payments due to authors with whom the PLR office has lost touch. (Completed and due for implementation, June 2005).

process for increased efficiency.

INGRES
2004 – 05 saw the successful migration and upgrade of PLR's RDBMS
system to a new server and the latest version of INGRES.

E-Registration
The new e-registration system was enhanced working closely with the
Author Services Team and plans are being made to fulfil author requests
to access their 'accounts' on-line.

IT Team
Darren Scrafton leads the team as IT Manager and is supported by
Helen Wadsworth, Technical Specialist.

Hardy Ferns

Michael Jeffers

Advisory Committee
Simon Brett, chair, reflects on the Committee's role

Objective 9
With DCMS, implement changes to PLR's legislation raising the maximum payment threshold to £6,600 and lowering the minimum threshold to £1. (Preparatory work completed; subject to Ministerial agreement, legislation to be changed by July 2005, with a start date of 2006-2007).

The PLR Advisory Committee exists to provide expert advice to the Secretary of State and the Registrar on aspects of the Scheme's operation. It does not share the Registrar's financial or executive responsibilities for PLR.

The Chairman and Members are appointed by the Secretary of State and are drawn from the fields of literature, libraries, and authors' rights. The Committee meets twice a year. The 2004 meetings took place in May (PLR, Stockton-on-Tees) and November (Society of Authors, London).

Changes to Membership 2004-05
Author Theresa Breslin stepped down from the Committee in November and Ministers appointed children's writer Tony Bradman in her place. Full details of the Committee's membership can be found in Annex A to the PLR Accounts.

You took over as Chair in August 2003. What was it that made you want to take this role on?

SB: As an author, I have always had a great affection for PLR. This is partly because the system has implemented the unarguable right of authors to benefit from library borrowings, and has also proved very generous to me. But I had also been impressed by the workings of the organisation, and really liked the people involved. So when the possibility of chairing the Advisory Committee arose, I thought, well maybe this is something I could do, and perhaps I should have a go. I was also intrigued by the continuing development of PLR, the refinement of the system in this country and its expansion into other countries. And I relished the prospect of working with the people of varied talents and backgrounds – writing, writers' organisations, libraries, the Civil Service – who all attend committee meetings.

What have been the most significant developments this year?

SB: As well as monitoring the very smooth day-to-day running of the existing scheme, the Advisory Committee has been concerned with the possibilities of expansion. It has long been felt that writers of reference books may have been missing out on PLR, and a working group has been set up to assess the feasibility of including them. We have recommended to DCMS Ministers that the capped top threshold for authors' payments be raised to £6,600, and that the minimum qualifying payment be lowered to £1. It is good to see that DCMS is progressing these proposals and that they should be introduced in 2006-07.

The contribution made by all of the Arts is frequently underestimated, and nowhere is that more true than in literature.

PLR is expanding its role through its collaborative work. How do you see authors and rights holders benefiting from this?

The contribution made by all of the Arts is frequently underestimated, and nowhere is that more true than in literature. DCMS figures show that creative industries are growing at a rate of 6% a year, as opposed to 3% for the rest of the economy. PLR can do much to help improve the profile of the writing profession, particularly through government initiatives in partnership with the DCMS and with public libraries through the Museums, Libraries and Archives Council (MLAC). All of this collaborative effort can help to bring a little more stability to that most precarious of professions – authorship.

Partnerships

PLR Working with Authors

PLR has spent 26 years serving authors in partnership with public libraries. The partnership has a long history. PLR exists due to the determination of writers who started campaigning in the 1950s for PLR to be recognised in law. In 1979 the Government passed the Public Lending Right Act.

We support the continuation and development of the Public Lending Right Scheme as a mechanism for encouraging and sustaining writing talent. Furthermore, the PLR Sheme contributes to the development and maintenance of important links between writers and libraries and, through libraries, to readers.

Conclusions & Recommendations, point 3 [ref. para. 27], the House of Commons Culture, Media and Sport Committee Public Libraries, Third Report of Session 2004-05, Volume 1, Report Together with Formal Minutes published by TSO, 10/03/05.

PLR continues to work collaboratively with writers. There are, on average, four authors on the DCMS-appointed Advisory Committee. PLR also works closely with authors' organisations to ensure that writers are aware of their right and that any concerns are communicated to the Registrar and Advisory Committee. Organisations include the Society of Authors, Authors' Licensing & Collecting Society (ALCS), The Writers' Guild of Great Britain, the Royal Society of Literature, and The Association of Authors' Agents.

In 2004-05 PLR supported the Scottish Arts Council in undertaking a survey of Scottish-based writers' earnings, and assisted ALCS in contacting authors for whom they hold monies.

Supporting Public Libraries and the Creative Economy

Authors and other rights holders make a vital contribution to Society, the knowledge economy and the creative industries.

PLR working with Public Libraries

PLR is the authors' legal right to payment and as such supports and enables creativity. It supports the Government's initiatives for the creative industries, and the contribution that reading and writing makes to social and educational development. By working in collaboration with its sponsoring department, DCMS, public libraries and a range of agencies that are committed to the future of public libraries, the enjoyment of reading and the development of readers, it can enhance the role of creators and writers.

Data sharing through LEWIS

" We have always had an interdependent relationship with public libraries and we are delighted at the opportunity that LEWIS presents to share our data," says Registrar, Jim Parker. "We are now refining the system with support from a working party made up of senior librarians and academics. Our aim is that the LEWIS system can be accessed and used by every library authority in the country. It has the potential to support our libraries in a variety of ways."

PLR Data – Monitoring Loans for Reader Development

Over the last 18 months, PLR has developed a close working relationship with The Reading Agency (TRA), an agency dedicated to developing readers nationally.

PLR's Sarah Beamson on how the relationship with TRA works

" During the year I've worked closely with TRA on a range of projects. Supplying our data to partner organisations is a growing part of my work. I liaise closely with their team and together we arrange to track any books included in a particular project or promotion such as the shortlist titles for the Orange Prize for Fiction.

" Our data is being put to really good use. The analysis I work on helps to establish just how effective a reading promotion is and shows how popular libraries, and particular titles, really are.

" So far we have only scraped the surface of PLR data use, but it's great to know we've developed something unique that's going to be so useful for libraries."

PLR has also supported the following promotions

WH Smith Prize	Richard and Judy books
Orange Prize	Radio 4 Book Club titles
British Book Award shortlist	BBC Page Turners
The Man Booker Prize	Daily Mail Book Club titles
Whitbread Book Awards	

PLR, the Private Sector and Public Libraries

PLR has also partnered TRA in their latest innovative project: *Reading Partners.* This brings together seven top UK publishers working in a public private sector parnership with public libraries. February 2005 saw the launch of *Borrowers Recommend* - a nationwide reading promotion in public libraries. Using PLR data to track various titles suggested by the participating publishers, 21 books were identified for inclusion. PLR data showed that these titles, although by relatively unknown or new authors, were sought out by library borrowers nationally.

"PLR staff have been unfailingly energetic and committed in working with us. It's a wonderful partnership that illuminates imaginative ways of using PLR's data."

Miranda McKearney, CEO, The Reading Agency.

PLR Celebrates its 25th Anniversary with Public Libraries
PLR enjoys a valued relationship with CILIP, the Chartered Institute of Library and Information Professionals. To celebrate the 25th Anniversary of the PLR Act, PLR and CILIP co-hosted a House of Commons reception. Hosted by Linda Perham MP the reception saw Members of Parliament and Peers mingling with some of the UK's best-known writers and illustrators to mark the occasion.

"We were delighted to have this opportunity to thank all those - authors, librarians and others - who have helped make PLR so successful over the last twenty five years."

Simon Brett, Chair, PLR Advisory Committee.

In October 2004, PLR hosted a 25th Anniversary reception at the Public Libraries Annual Conference, Newcastle. This was an opportunity for PLR to show their appreciation of public libraries' support over the last two and half decades.

In support of the wider agenda
PLR also works with a range of agencies which share, in a variety of ways, a central interest in public libraries, the creative industries, and authors' rights in support of the Government's wider agenda. These

include The Chartered Institute of Public Finance and Accountancy (CIPFA), The Society of Chief Librarians (SCL), The Library Information Statistics Unit, Loughborough University (LISU) and Book Marketing Ltd (BML).

Maisie Jeffery, 9, (left): Vampire Plagues by Sebastian Rook

HARBERTONFORD Jane Jeffery, (second left), weekend break, Cornwall: The Jonah by James Herbert

HARBERTONFORD Kara Jeffery, 9: Double Act by Jacqueline Wilson

Communication

PLR has a proactive strategy to ensure that the widest number of people possible, from Government ministers through to young readers and aspiring writers, understand what it does and why it matters.

The Annual Media Campaign 2005
Each February PLR releases information about its top lending authors and titles. This year, for the first time, PLR was able to release a much wider range of information on the nation's borrowing habits thanks to the new LEWIS data service.

Hip Lit – suddenly books are popular again
Sunderland Echo

For the second year running the spotlight fell on children's writer, Jacqueline Wilson, as the nation's most-borrowed author with over two million loans.

Intense media interest in Jacqueline Wilson led to interviews for television, radio and newspapers. Novelist Josephine Cox was interviewed with PLR's Chair, Simon Brett, on BBC Radio Four's Today programme and the LEWIS data generated excellent regional coverage as local papers picked up on local reading habits.

The Registrar undertakes a busy schedule of speaking engagements every year, at home and abroad. In 2004 – 05 he provided best practice advice to aspiring PLR countries. The events attended were held in Budapest, Alexandria, Rome, Dublin, Slovenia, Munich and Copenhagen. He also spoke at events in the UK organised by the Romantic Novelists Association, the Garden Writers Guild and the Association of Authors' Agents.

ASPRINGTON Francis Phillips, 2: Mog in the Garden by Judith Kerr

ASHPRINGTON Jessica Phillips, 12: Up and Down in the Dales by Gervase Phinn.

International

PLR plays an active role in encouraging the recognition of PLR internationally as fair reward for authors for the use of their works in libraries.

The 1992 European Directive required all EU member states to implement PLR schemes. Since 1995, the UK scheme has taken a leading role in helping other nations to establish PLR. Working in partnership with the European Commission, the European Writers' Congress and other international agencies, the Registrar helped to run a series of seminars aimed at assisting the development of new schemes in EU member states.

In 2004 PLR systems in the new member states of Slovenia, Estonia, Latvia and Lithuania all got off the ground. However, 2004 also saw the European Commission refer Italy, Luxembourg, Spain, Ireland and Portugal to the European Court of Justice for failing to implement PLR legislation.

Rome Seminar

PLR's European Specialist, Janice Forbes, reports on the PLR seminar for new member states:

" My work is divided between publicising our scheme across the EU, to make sure authors know they are eligible for PLR here in the UK, and supporting the Registrar in offering technical advice to the newer EU countries looking to set up schemes.

" For Rome we collaborated with the Norwegians to offer a seminar for the new East European member states. The aim was to share good practice and offer support and advice.

" It was great just to be there. We'd recently helped Slovenia and

Estonia set up their systems and it felt good to hear how they were doing. Of course, there's still lots to do before every member state has a scheme but it's nice to be able to share our experiences and give advice whenever we can."

Preparations for the Berlin International PLR Conference 2005

This year the Registrar, as co-ordinator of the International PLR Network, has supported preparations for the next International PLR Conference. Berlin 2005 will mark the 10th anniversary of the biennial meetings. The first was held in the UK in 1995 since when the Registrar has assisted with the continuing programme of conferences.

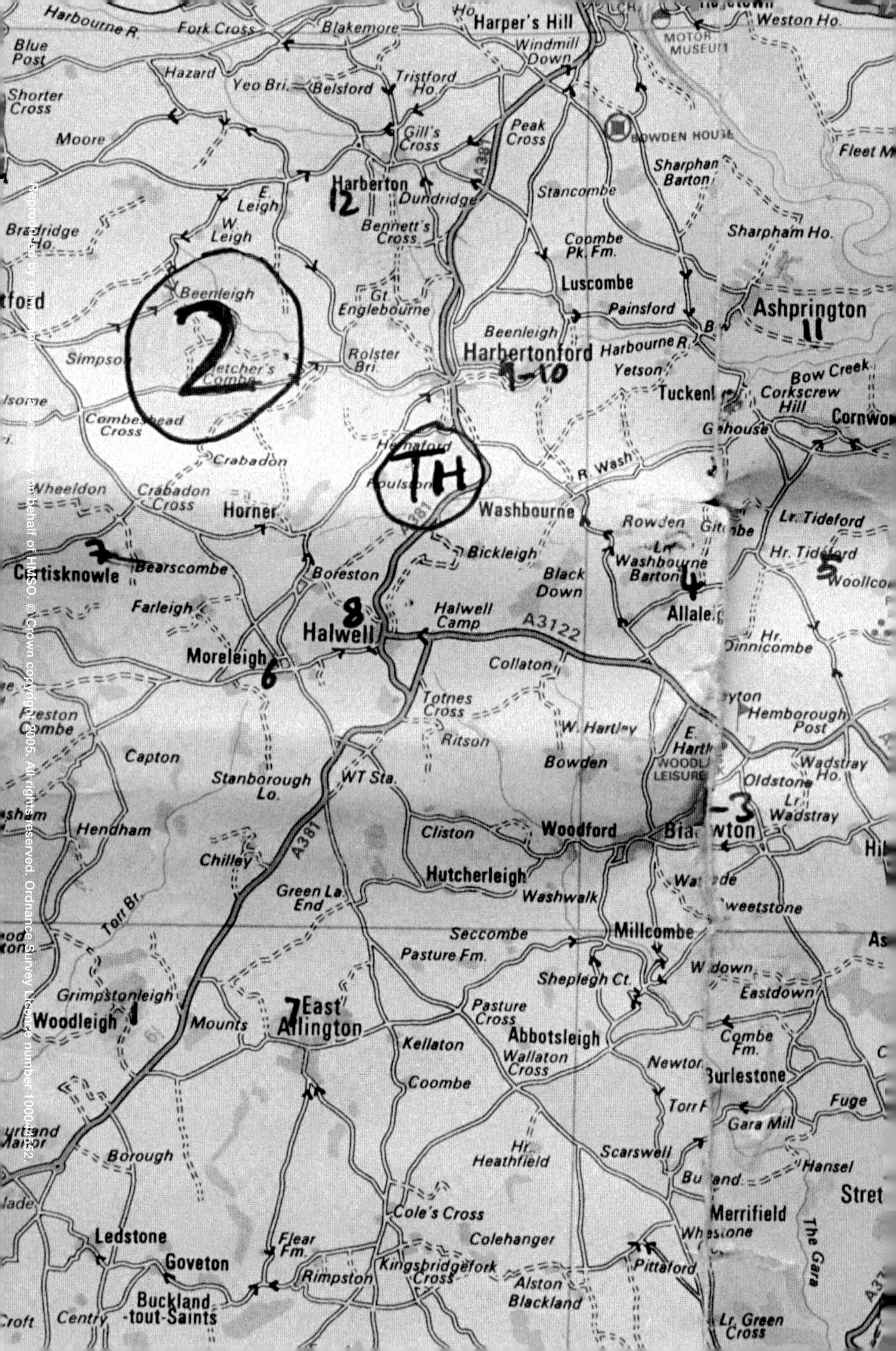
Harbourne R.
Fork Cross
Blakemore
Harper's Hill
Weston Ho.
Motor Museum
Blue Post
Windmill Down
Hazard
Yeo Bri.
Belsford
Tristford Ho.
Shorter Cross
Moore
Gill's Cross
Peak Cross
Bowden House
Fleet Mill
Harberton
12
Dundridge
A381
Stancombe
Sharpham Barton
E. Leigh
W. Leigh
Bradridge Ho.
Bennett's Cross
Coombe Pk. Fm.
Sharpham Ho.
Beenleigh
Gt. Englebourne
Luscombe
Painsford
Ashprington
2
Simpson
Fletcher's Combe
Rolster Bri.
Beenleigh
Harbertonford
1-10
Harbourne R.
Yetson
11
Bow Creek
Corkscrew Hill
Combeshead Cross
Hernaford
TH
Poulston
Crabadon
R. Wash
Wheeldon
Crabadon Cross
Horner
Washbourne
Rowden
Lr. Tideford
Bickleigh
Hr. Tideford
Curtisknowle
Bearscombe
Boreston
Black Down
Washbourne Barton
4
5
Farleigh
8
Halwell Camp
Halwell
A3122
Moreleigh
6
Collaton
Hr. Dinnicombe
Preston Combe
Totnes Cross
Hemborough Post
Ritson
W. Hartley
Capton
Stanborough Lo.
WT Sta.
Bowden
Woodland Leisure
Wadstray Ho.
Oldstone
Lr. Wadstray
3
Hendham
Cliston
Woodford
Chilley
Hutcherleigh
Washwalk
Green La. End
Torr Br.
Seccombe
Millcombe
Pasture Fm.
Shepleigh Ct.
Eastdown
Grimpstonleigh
Woodleigh
Mounts
7
East Allington
Pasture Cross
Abbotsleigh
Kellaton
Wallaton Cross
Newton
Combe Fm.
Burlestone
Coombe
Fuge
Gara Mill
Hr. Heathfield
Scarswell
Borough
Hansel
Stret
Merrifield
Cole's Cross
Colehanger
Ledstone
Goveton
Flear Fm.
Kingsbridgefork Cross
Rimpston
Alston
Blackland
Pittaford
The Gara
Buckland -tout-Saints
Centry
Lr. Green Cross

MORELEIGH Liz Redshaw: Hunter's Moon by Garry Kilworth

Hardy Ferns

...IAGE
...ANTS

IN

GARDEN

DESIGN

...ael Jefferson-Brown

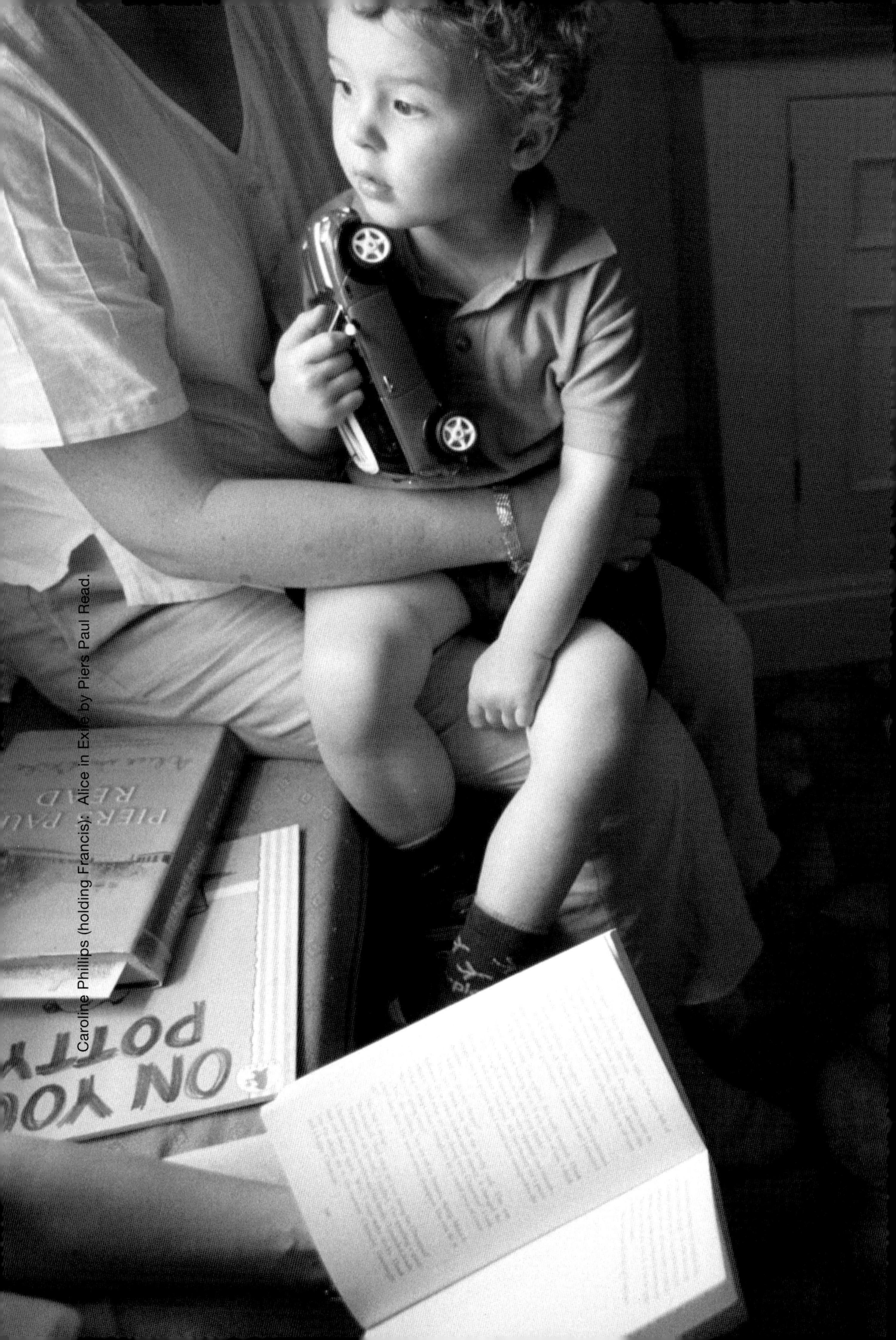

Caroline Phillips (holding Francis): Alice in Exile by Piers Paul Read.

Jonathan Gibbs

enthuses about LEWIS and the potential benefits on offer to Public Libraries

Public librarians thrive within partnerships. We've long prided ourselves on our links with other libraries; that ability to pull a rare literary rabbit out of the hat to the amazement of our users. Computers have provided us with the means to speed service delivery.

Bibliographic tools have also changed immeasurably since I first laid eyes on a microfiche. Now web-based catalogues for both libraries and on-line book suppliers are commonplace and endow the public with a degree of stock knowledge that may on occasion be better than our own. With ever more constraints upon both our time and budgets, librarians require a

At its most fundamental level,
LEWIS data on loans will allow
authorities participating in the PLR
sample to benefit directly from their
involvement.

means of focussing knowledge to ensure that we spend wisely and that
our stock remains relevant.

PLR's LEWIS database will I believe enhance those partnerships libraries
have worked hard to create. At its most fundamental level, LEWIS data on
loans will allow authorities participating in the PLR sample to benefit
directly from their involvement. Librarians will in turn gain a greater
understanding of the vital work of the PLR scheme and its importance to
authors. In this new century the knowledge that authors and librarians are
inter-dependent, and that neither group could survive without the other,
must be central to the survival of public library services in this country.

The most fundamental partnership any library has is with its users. In the
last few years people have been returning to libraries. The LEWIS database
can assist in that partnership – giving us information about most-borrowed
items in a given area of stock within seconds. And because results from
the database can be assessed nationally, on a regional basis, or for a
single authority, cooperation between authorities can be enhanced.

'I'm looking for something...' is a phrase dreaded by most librarians. Our
hearts sink as we realise that the person in front of us will be relying
entirely upon our critical faculties for their choice. With subject indexing by
book industry codes, we can quickly see from LEWIS what is popular
within a subject area. There is no substitute for stock knowledge, but
LEWIS can augment that knowledge, providing those on the other side of

There is no substitute for stock knowledge, but LEWIS can augment that knowledge, providing those on the other side of the enquiry desk, with a wealth of data.

The most fundamental partnership any library has is with its users. The LEWIS database can assist in that partnership – giving us information about most-borrowed items in a given area of stock within seconds.

the enquiry desk, with a wealth of data. Now if PLR could find a way to resolve that other perennial cry from users – '…It was a big blue book and I saw it last Thursday…'.

I work in a busy London library and I was fortunate to see LEWIS demonstrated earlier this year. My colleagues learned to avoid me as I went round enthusing about its potential. But I believe that enthusiasm will be shared by anyone who appreciates what LEWIS can offer - a stock tool to assist in editing, as a mechanism for ensuring the relevance of our own material, as a means of necessary introspection. It's a resource we have never had the opportunity to employ properly and I cannot wait to use it.

Jonathan Gibbs 2005
Jonathan Gibbs is Operations and IT Librarian at the Barbican Library, Corporation of London Libraries

Tony Bradman,

who joined the Advisory Committee in 2004, talks about the importance and value of rights for children's authors

There are very few fixed points in the working lives of most writers. Inspiration itself is notoriously fickle, editors and publishing houses come and go, sometimes with disconcerting speed, books that have been selling well for years suddenly go out of print and the royalty cheques dry up.

But it isn't just about the money. Knowing that books of yours are still being borrowed can give you a very warm glow inside, even in the darkest days of winter.

You can, however, always rely on your PLR. I'm pretty sure I first registered with the scheme in 1987, and got my first payment in February 1988. Ever since, it's been the one fixed point in the ups and downs of my writing life, the statement arriving at just the right time of year, in the gloomy weeks between Christmas and January 31st, when freelancers have to pay their tax, the actual payment turning up soon after (phew!).

But it isn't just about the money, as any writer will tell you. The statements make fascinating reading, and knowing that books of yours are still being borrowed, sometimes long after they've gone out of print, can give you a very warm glow inside, even in the darkest days of winter. A high level of loans on an out-of-print book also provides you with a terrific excuse to berate your publisher, something most writers enjoy.

There's an added bonus, too. I've always found the staff at the PLR offices in Stockton to be very friendly and efficient, and concerned to get things right for authors. Unlike most editors, they're rarely 'in a meeting'. So I was delighted when I was appointed to the PLR Advisory Committee. It's great to get away from the desk and that awful blank screen from time to time; even better if it's for a meeting with other people who are taking care of authors' interests, and readers' interests too. I've been to two meetings so far and found them to be very business-like (Simon Brett is an excellent chair), the subjects discussed fascinating.

As a children's writer, I find I have plenty to say. Young families and

I've always found the staff at the PLR offices in Stockton to be very friendly and efficient, and concerned to get things right for authors.

Young families and children make up a large chunk of the total number of borrowers. I'm keen to make sure their interests continue to be well served.

children make up a large chunk of the total number of borrowers, as PLR's list of most-borrowed authors reveals, with children's favourite Jacqueline Wilson currently top of the league. I'm keen to make sure their interests continue to be well served, and also that the contribution of children's writers to our cultural life continues to be recognised and rewarded.

I'm also very keen to make sure those statements and payments keep coming in the deepest, darkest days of winter. Publishers might come and go, the Muse might forget to come and pay me quite as many visits as she should – but I hope that Public Lending Right will go on forever…

Tony Bradman 2005
Tony Bradman is a children's writer and Member of the PLR Advisory Committee

PLR Central Fund Account
for the year ended
31 March 2005

PUBLIC LENDING RIGHT
CENTRAL FUND ACCOUNT 2004 - 2005

FOREWORD

These are the accounts for the twenty second year of the Public Lending Right (PLR) Central Fund and cover the annual payments due to authors at 31 March 2005.

History and Statutory Background

The Public Lending Right Act 1979 established a right for authors to receive remuneration from public funds in respect of their books lent out from public libraries. The calculation of library loans is estimated from a sample of public libraries where issues are recorded electronically and processed by local authority computers before transmission to the Registrar's computer at Stockton-on-Tees: for the twenty second year's calculations the number of library authorities in the sample was 38.

The details of eligible books, eligible authors, and payment calculations are set out in The Public Lending Right Scheme 1982, as amended in 1983, 1984, 1988, 1989 and 1990. The consolidated text appears in Statutory Instrument 1990 No 2360. Further amendments were made in Statutory Instruments 1991 No 2618, 1993 No 799, 1996 No 3237, 1997 No 1576, 1998 No 1218, 1999 Nos 420, 905, 3304, 2000 Nos 933, 3319, 2001 No 3984, 2002 No 3123, 2003 No 839, 2003 No 3045, 2004 No 1258, 2004 No 3128.

The Public Lending Right Advisory Committee advises the Secretary of State for Culture, Media and Sport and the Registrar on the operation of the Scheme but has no formal responsibility for the management of PLR. Appointments to the Committee are made by the Secretary of State. Details of the Committee's membership at 31 March 2005 are provided in Annex A.

Review of Activities

The twenty second year's operations are described in the PLR Annual Report which includes the statutory report on the operation of the Scheme laid before Parliament by the Secretary of State for Culture, Media and Sport. Following consultation with the Department for Culture, Media and Sport a separate Operating and Financial Review (OFR) of the Scheme's activities during 2004-2005 are not included in the Annual Report on the basis that all key aspects of the OFR are covered below in this Foreword.

a) Operating Charges

Restructuring of the Corporate Services Team to meet the requirements of the 2002 Quinquennial Review resulted in the redundancy costs noted under Staff Costs. But the main focus of our work in modernising our administration of the Scheme and improving the service that we provide to authors and libraries continues to be in the area of e-business. E-registration, introduced last year to enable authors to register with PLR on-line, grew in popularity. By the year end 50% of first-time applications for registration were received on-line via the PLR web-site. All 38 library authorities in the PLR sample are now providing loans data by e-mail thus reducing costs and simplifying supply procedures. The bulk of the work associated with automating records of 'on-hold' payments (ie where contact has been lost with authors to whom money is due) and further integration of PLR's book registration and payment systems has largely been completed and will shortly be up and running.

b) Payments to Authors

PLR's core funding from DCMS was increased to £7.381 million (£7.201 million in 2003-2004). On the basis of the increased funding, it proved possible to increase the level of the rate per loan for the February 2005 payments to authors to 5.26 pence, the highest figure to date (4.85 pence in 2003-2004). A total sum of £6,536,539 was made available from the Central Fund for paying out to 18,666 authors. 81% of the Fund was distributed in payments of £500 or more.

18,666 authors and assignees (18,783 in 2003-2004) qualified for payments. The numbers of authors in the various payment categories were as follows:

	Twenty Second Year	Twenty First Year
Authors Earning:		
£6,000.00	285	274
£5,000.00 - £5,999.99	70	81
£2,500.00 £4,999.99	376	350
£1,000.00 £2,499.99	783	767
£500.00 £999.99	911	910
£100.00 £499.99	3,826	3,875
£50.00 - £99.99	2,518	2,545
£5.00 - £49.99	9,897	9,981
	18,666	18,783
Expenditure	6,536,539	6,411,616

Expenditure includes £38,600 still to be paid at the year end. These authors' addresses are unknown to PLR, or their assignees have not made probate claims. A further £5,000 is a separate provision which is used to supplement the central fund. There were 15,011 (14,079 in 2003-2004) authors whose books earned no payment.

An analysis of the distribution of money for the twenty second year to authors by payment category shows:

	£	%
£6,000.00	1,715,774	26.25
£5,000.00 - £5,999.99	387,979	5.93
£2,500.00 - £4,999.99	1,319,779	20.20
£1,000.00 - £2,499.99	1,221,545	18.69
£500.00 - £999.99	647,892	9.91
£100.00 - £499.99	871,383	13.33
£50.00 - £99.99	180,118	2.76
£5.00 - £49.99	192,069	2.93
		100.00

c) Strengths, Weaknesses and Risks

We place much emphasis on maintaining cost-effective systems, remaining open to modernisation and improvement, and being responsive to authors' needs and concerns. We feel that the success of our staff in each of these areas is a source of great strength for the PLR organisation. For example, the high regard in which the Author Services team is held came through strongly in the 100% satisfaction rating received from authors for the service provided by the team over the last year. Risk management too is now central to our planning systems and PLR's Risk Register is kept under continuous review by the Registrar and his management team. Key risks currently include the implications for the Scheme of the impending change in the international ISBN system with the move from 10 digit to 13 digit ISBNs; the dangers of inadequate business continuity planning and 'initiative overload'; the threat to IT systems posed by computer viruses. To mitigate these risks PLR has reviewed its systems for project planning and disaster recovery, has set up a project team to tackle the ISBN issue, and works hard at building regular and reliable communications with the third parties on whom it relies for the provision of data and other services.

Fixed Assets

No land or buildings are owned. No funds are accumulated for the replacement of other assets. Future replacement will need to be financed from funds voted in the year of acquisition.

Movements on fixed assets are set out in note 6 to the financial statements.

Payment of Creditors

The Registrar adheres to the Government-wide standard for payment of bills by aiming to settle all bills within thirty days. In 2004-2005, 99% of creditor invoices were paid within 30 days of being received (2003-2004, 95%). Every effort is also made by PLR to effect payments to authors on the annual date fixed by the Registrar. However, as a result of failure by authors to notify PLR of changes in address or bank details, and of other circumstances outside the control of the Registrar, it may not always be possible to make payment. In such cases, the Registrar is required to hold payments as debts due to the authors concerned for up to six years during which period all reasonable efforts are made by PLR to effect payment.

Superannuation

The PCSPS is a "pay-as-you-go" statutory unfunded pension scheme. In accordance with Section 40 of the Social Security Pensions Act 1975 such schemes are exempted from the need to set up funds. The liability to pay pensions is underwritten by an understanding that in accordance with existing legislation, in particular the Superannuation Act 1972, the Government is obliged to provide benefits to members of such schemes in accordance with their respective rules.

Results and Appropriations

The Fund is distributed after deduction of the Registrar's remuneration, administrative costs, and payments to local authorities. The surplus for the year was £18,324. As a result, the Central Fund ended the year with a surplus carried forward of £23,033.

Future developments

Our primary function will continue to be to administer the PLR Scheme efficiently, cost-effectively and fairly, with the emphasis, as ever, on providing authors with the best service possible and meeting the targets for running costs set by DCMS through our Funding Agreement and Efficiency Delivery Plan. Additionally, we shall be working with DCMS to get parliamentary agreement to changes to the Scheme's minimum and maximum payment thresholds for implementation in 2006-07.

In terms of modernisation the main thrust of our project work continues to be in the area of e-business. The first phases of e-registration for authors and development of the LEWIS loans database for use by the public library community are now complete and have been very well received by their target audiences. There is much enthusiasm in both constituencies for our plans for the next phases of each project. We will aim to resume work on these following completion in the coming year of work on our electronic records management (EDRM) system and a major overhaul of our systems required as a result of the book trade's decision to extend the length of ISBNs from ten to thirteen digits.

Registrar's Salary and Superannuation

As specified in the Act, the Registrar's own remuneration and superannuation costs are charged directly against the £7,472,500 grant due to be made available. As they are not made from the Central Fund, they do not appear in these accounts. A reconciliation to the grant received is shown at note 2. In 2004-2005 the total deduction was £69,538 (2003-2004 £65,704).

Staffing Matters

The Registrar of Public Lending Right is committed to promoting effective consultation and communications with his staff. PLR's Corporate and Author Services Teams have regular staff meetings at which matters relating to PLR's activities are discussed. Additionally, staff are briefed on matters discussed at senior management and planning meetings. PLR recognises the Public and Commercial Services Union for the purpose of collective bargaining.

The Registrar of Public Lending Right makes every effort to employ disabled people in suitable employment and gives full and fair consideration to applications for employment of disabled people.

Organisation

The PLR Act 1979 gives the Registrar sole corporate responsibility for the PLR Scheme. The PLR Advisory Committee provides advice to the Registrar and DCMS Ministers on aspects of the Scheme's operation. For the last two years, the day-to-day management of the Scheme has been undertaken by Author and Corporate Services teams reporting through Team Leaders to the Assistant Registrar. This devolution of responsibility enables the Registrar to concentrate on strategic and developmental issues.

Performance Indicators

As part of the Funding Agreement with the Department for Culture, Media and Sport, the Registrar of Public Lending Right has identified one financial measure related to the organisation's aims. Details of actual result against target are set out in note 19.

The Euro

The activities of Public Lending Right are mainly within the United Kingdom. Exposure to transactions denominated in the Euro occurs in respect of authors resident overseas. These are treated no differently from transactions in any foreign currency. Public Lending Right's systems are accordingly already Euro-enabled.

Auditors

The audit of the Public Lending Right Central Fund accounts is carried out by the Comptroller and Auditor General under section 2(6) of the Public Lending Right Act 1979.

J G Parker
Registrar

6 July 2005

Annex A

PLR Advisory Committee

The members of the Advisory Committee during the year were:

Mr Simon Brett (Chairman)

Dr James Parker (Registrar of PLR)

Mr Tony Bradman *(Appointed 8 November 2004)*

Ms Theresa Breslin *(Resigned November 2004)*

Ms Gill Coleridge

Mr Rob Froud

Dr Maggie Gee

Ms Miranda McKearney

Dr Barry Turner

Other than the Registrar, none of the Advisory Committee members received any remuneration from PLR.

Registrar's Remuneration Committee

Mr Simon Brett (Chairman)

Ms Gill Coleridge

Mr Mark Le Fanu

PLR Audit Committee

The members of the Audit Committee during the year were:

Mr Mike Dewsnap (Chairman)

Mr Mike Duffy

Dr James Parker

RESPONSIBILITIES OF THE REGISTRAR AND DCMS ACCOUNTING OFFICER

Under section 2(6) of the Public Lending Right Act 1979, the Registrar is required to prepare a statement of accounts for the Public Lending Right Central Fund for each financial year in the form and on the basis determined by the Secretary of State for Culture, Media and Sport, with the consent of the Treasury. The accounts are prepared on an accruals basis and must show a true and fair view of the Central Fund's state of affairs at the year end and of its income and expenditure and cash flows for the financial year.

In preparing the accounts the Registrar is required to:

- observe the accounts direction issued[1] by the Secretary of State, including the relevant accounting and disclosure requirements, and apply suitable accounting policies on a consistent basis;

- make judgements and estimates on a reasonable basis;

- state whether applicable accounting standards have been followed, and disclose and explain any material departures in the financial statements; and

- prepare the financial statements on the going concern basis, unless it is inappropriate to presume that the Central Fund will continue in operation.

The Accounting Officer of the Department for Culture, Media and Sport is the Accounting Officer for payments to the Registrar.

Under Section 2(1) of the Public Lending Right Act 1979, the Central Fund is placed under the management and control of the Registrar who is also responsible for the keeping of proper records. The Accounting Officer of the Department for Culture, Media and Sport has designated the Registrar as the Accounting Officer for the use of, and expenditure from, the Central Fund. As Accounting Officer he has overall responsibility for the propriety and regularity of the Public Lending Right Central Fund finances for which he is answerable to Parliament and for the keeping of proper records. His responsibilities as Accounting Officer are set out in the Accounting Officer's Memorandum issued by the Treasury and published in Government Accounting.

[1] A copy of the accounts direction can be obtained from the following address: Public Lending Right, Richard House, Sorbonne Close, Stockton-on-Tees, TS17 6DA.

J G Parker
Registrar

6 July 2005

STATEMENT OF INTERNAL CONTROL

As Accounting Officer, I have responsibility for maintaining a sound system of internal control that supports the achievement of PLR policies, aims and objectives, whilst safeguarding the public funds and assets for which I am personally responsible, in accordance with the responsibilities assigned to me in Government Accounting and ensuring compliance with the requirements of PLR's Management Statement and Financial Memorandum.

The system of internal control is designed to manage rather than eliminate the risk of failure to achieve policies, aims and objectives; it can therefore only provide reasonable and not absolute assurance of effectiveness.

The system of internal control takes account of Treasury guidance and is based on an ongoing process designed to identify the principal risks to the achievement of PLR policies, aims and objectives, to evaluate the nature and extent of those risks and to manage them efficiently, effectively and economically.

Following some further risk management training last year from our internal auditors our system has been firmly embedded in our operating systems throughout the year. As part of our approach we now identify our objectives and risks and have determined a control strategy for each of the significant risks. A risk management policy document has been sent to all staff setting out PLR's risk strategy.

The Registrar's management team has been reviewing risk management and internal control on a regular basis during the year and there has been a full risk and control assessment before reporting on the year ending 31 March 2005.

PLR employs internal auditors who operate to standards defined in the Government Internal Audit Standards. They submit regular reports which include an independent opinion on the adequacy and effectiveness of PLR's system of internal control together with the recommendations for improvement.

The Audit Committee receives periodic reports from PLR's internal auditors concerning internal control. The internal auditors work closely with PLR's managers on the steps needed to manage risks in their areas of responsibility.

My review of the effectiveness of the system of internal control is informed by the work of the internal auditors and PLR's executive managers who have responsibility for the development and maintenance of the internal control framework, and comments made by the external auditors in their management letter and other reports. I am also guided in this regard by the Audit Committee which advises me on the effectiveness of PLR's internal control systems. In addition to overall annual audit assurance and regular block reports on which to base its advice, the Committee receives copies of PLR's Corporate Plan and other strategy documents; details of key risks and lists of other evidence used by the Registrar to assess the robustness of PLR control systems; and regular progress reports on PLR's implementation of outstanding audit recommendations.

In light of the evidence available to me, I believe that PLR has had all the necessary risk management and review processes in place throughout 2004-2005.

J G Parker
Registrar

6 July 2005

PUBLIC LENDING RIGHT CENTRAL FUND

The Certificate and Report of the Comptroller and Auditor General to the Houses of Parliament

I certify that I have audited the financial statements on pages 97 to 109 under the Public Lending Right Act 1979. These financial statements have been prepared under the historic cost convention as modified by the revaluation of certain fixed assets and the accounting policies set out on page 100.

Respective responsibilities of the Registrar, the Accounting Officer of the Department for Culture, Media and Sport, and the Auditor

As described on page 94, the Accounting Officer of the Department for Culture, Media and Sport has responsibility for payments into the Public Lending Right Central Fund and to the Registrar. The Registrar, as Accounting Officer for the use of and expenditure from the Public Lending Right Central Fund, is responsible for the preparation of financial statements in accordance with the Public Lending Right Act 1979 and directions made thereunder by the Secretary of State for Culture, Media and Sport and for ensuring the regularity of financial transactions. The Registrar is also responsible for the preparation of the Foreword. I have regard to the standards and guidance issued by the Auditing Practices Board and the ethical guidance applicable to the auditing profession.

I report my opinion as to whether the financial statements give a true and fair view, and are properly prepared in accordance with the Public Lending Right Act 1979 and directions made by the Secretary of State for Culture, Media and Sport thereunder, and whether in all material respects the expenditure and income have been applied to the purposes intended by Parliament and the financial transactions conform to the authorities which govern them. I also report, if in my opinion, the Foreword on pages 89 to 93, is not consistent with the financial statements; if the Public Lending Right has not kept proper accounting records; or if I have not received all the information and explanations I require for my audit.

I read the other information contained in the Annual Report and consider whether it is consistent with the audited financial statements. I consider the implications for my certificate if I become aware of any apparent misstatements or material inconsistencies with the financial statements.

I review whether the statement on page 95 reflects the Public Lending Right's compliance with Treasury's guidance 'Corporate Governance: statement on internal control'. I report if it does not meet the requirements specified by Treasury, or if the statement is misleading or inconsistent with other information I am aware of from my audit of the financial statements. I am not required to consider, nor have I considered whether the Accounting Officer's Statement on Internal Control covers all risks and controls. I am also not required to form an opinion on the effectiveness of the Public Lending Right's corporate governance procedures or its risk and control procedures.

Basis of audit opinion

I conducted my audit in accordance with United Kingdom Auditing Standards issued by the Auditing Practices Board. An audit includes examination, on a test basis, of evidence relevant to the amounts and disclosures and regularity of the financial transactions included in the financial statements. It also includes an assessment of the significant estimates and judgements made by the Registrar in the preparation of the financial statements, and of whether the accounting policies are appropriate to the Fund's circumstances, consistently applied and adequately disclosed.

I planned and performed my audit so as to obtain all the information and explanations which I considered necessary in order to provide me with sufficient evidence to give reasonable assurance that the financial statements are free from material misstatement, whether caused by error, or by fraud or other irregularity and that, in all material respects, the expenditure and income have been applied to the purposes intended by Parliament and the financial transactions conform to the authorities which govern them. In forming my opinion I also evaluated the overall adequacy of the presentation of information in the financial statements.

Opinion

In my opinion:

■ the financial statements give a true and fair view of the state of affairs of the Public Lending Right Central Fund at 31 March 2005 and of the surplus, total recognised gains and losses and cash flows for the year then ended and have been properly prepared in accordance with the Public Lending Right Act 1979 and with the directions made thereunder by the Secretary of State for Culture, Media and Sport.

■ in all material respects the expenditure and income have been applied to the purposes intended by Parliament and the financial transactions conform to the authorities which govern them.

I have no observations to make on these financial statements.

John Bourn
Comptroller and Auditor General
12 July 2005

National Audit Office
157-197 Buckingham Palace Road
Victoria
London SW1W 9SP

PUBLIC LENDING RIGHT CENTRAL FUND

INCOME AND EXPENDITURE ACCOUNT
FOR THE YEAR ENDED 31 MARCH 2005

INCOME	Notes	£	2004-05 £	2003-04 £
HM Government Grant	2	7,402,962		7,095,296
Income in respect of pension transfer to PCSPS	2	-		93,540
Income in respect of accrued superannuation liability contributions	2	-		52,359
			7,402,962	7,241,195
Less: Transferred to Government grant reserve	3		(11,361)	-
Other Operating Income	4		18,675	29,503
Total income available to PLR Central Fund			7,410,276	7,270,698
EXPENDITURE				
Staff Costs	5	(460,478)		(377,475)
Depreciation	6	(18,531)		(24,315)
Other Operating Charges	7	(393,471)		(373,289)
Public Lending Right to Authors		(6,536,539)		(6,411,616)
			7,409,019	7,186,695
Operating Surplus	8		1,257	84,003
Income from other activities - interest receivable	22	15,199		8,949
- pension account	9	847		822
			16,046	9,771
Surplus on ordinary activities before taxation			17,303	93,774
Corporation Tax	22		1,021	(1,700)
Notional Cost of Capital	17		772	617
Surplus after Notional Costs			19,096	92,691
Reversal of Notional Costs			(772)	(617)
Surplus for the Financial Year			18,324	92,074
Retained Surplus/(Deficit) brought forward			4,709	(87,365)
Retained Surplus carried forward			23,033	4,709

The income and expenditure relate to continuing activities.

The Fund has no recognised gains and losses other than those above and consequently no separate statement of total recognised gains and losses has been presented.

The notes on pages 100 to 109 form part of these accounts.

PUBLIC LENDING RIGHT CENTRAL FUND

BALANCE SHEET AS AT 31 MARCH 2005

	Notes	2004-05 £	2004-05 £	2003-04 £
FIXED ASSETS				
Tangible Assets	6		11,071	18,241
CURRENT ASSETS				
Debtors	10	24,958		17,563
Cash at Bank and In Hand		147,808		118,347
		172,766		135,910
CREDITORS				
Amounts falling due within one year	11	(140,125)		(123,441)
Net Current Assets			32,641	12,469
Total Assets Less Current Liabilities			43,712	30,710
FINANCED BY:				
CAPITAL AND RESERVES				
Government Grant Reserve	3		11,071	18,241
Public Lending Right Reserve	12		9,608	7,760
Income and Expenditure Account			23,033	4,709
			43,712	30,710

The notes on pages 100 to 109 form part of these accounts.

J G Parker
Registrar

6 July 2005

98

PUBLIC LENDING RIGHT CENTRAL FUND

CASH FLOW STATEMENT

FOR THE YEAR ENDED 31 MARCH 2005

	Notes	2004-05 £	2003-04 £
Net Cash Inflow/(Outflow) from Operating Activities	13	13,058	(22,497)
NET CASH INFLOW FROM Returns on Investment and Servicing of Finance Interest Received	22	15,114	11,025
Taxation Corporation Tax Paid		442	(442)
NET CASH OUTFLOW FROM Capital Expenditure and Financial Investment Purchase of Fixed Assets	6	(11,361)	-
NET CASH INFLOW FROM Pensions Account	9	847	822
NET CASH INFLOW FROM Financing Government Grant Applied to Capital	3	11,361	-
Increase/(Decrease) in Cash	14	29,461	(11,092)

The notes on pages 100 to 109 form part of these accounts.

NOTES TO THE ACCOUNTS AT 31 MARCH 2005

NOTE 1   ACCOUNTING POLICIES

ACCOUNTING CONVENTION

These accounts are prepared under the historical cost convention, as modified by the revaluation of certain fixed assets. Without limiting the information given, the accounts meet the accounting and disclosure requirements of the Companies Act and Accounting Standards issued or adopted by the Accounting Standards Board so far as those requirements are appropriate.

ASSETS AND DEPRECIATION

Fixed assets are accounted for using modified historic cost accounting. However, adjustments to the net book value are only made where material and no such adjustments were made in 2004-2005.

Depreciation is provided on all tangible fixed assets at rates calculated to write off the cost or valuation, less the estimated residual value of each asset, evenly over its expected useful life. Items under £1,000 are written off in the year of purchase. Items over £1,000 are depreciated evenly over 3 years for computer equipment and 5 years for fixtures and fittings.

VALUE ADDED TAX

PLR is outside the scope of VAT.

HM GOVERNMENT GRANT

The capital element of the Grant from the Department for Culture, Media and Sport is credited to a Government Grant Reserve and released to revenue over the expected useful life of the relevant assets. The revenue element of the Grant is credited to income in the year to which it relates.

LEASES

Costs relating to operating leases are charged to the income and expenditure account over the life of the lease.

PENSIONS

Past and present employees are covered by the provisions of the Principal Civil Service Pension Schemes (PCSPS). The defined benefit elements of the schemes are unfunded and are non-contributory except in respect of dependant's benefits. The Central Fund recognises the expected costs of these elements on a systematic and rational basis over the period during which it benefits from the employees' services by payment to the PCSPS of amounts calculated on an accruing basis. Liability for payment of future benefits is a charge on the PCSPS.

NOTIONAL COSTS

In accordance with Treasury guidance, notional costs of capital (calculated at 3.5% of the average capital employed) are charged in the Income and Expenditure Account in arriving at the "Surplus after Notional Costs". These are reversed so that no provision is included in the balance sheet.

NOTE 2   HM GOVERNMENT GRANT

	2004-05	2003-04
	£	£
Grant for PLR (DCMS RfR1)	7,472,500	7,306,899
LESS Registrar's Costs	(69,538)	(65,704)
Grant to Central Fund	7,402,962	7,241,195

For 2004-2005 the government grant announced in the 2002 Spending Review was £7,381,000. A further £51,500 has been provided by DCMS to meet PLR's increased superannuation charges following the move of staff to the PCSPS. In addition to this year's allocation, £40,000 was received from DCMS from the 2003-04 allocation which was not drawn down in that year.

The Registrar's Costs comprise the salary and National Insurance payments of the present Registrar. The Registrar's pension scheme is unfunded.

The Registrar's contract was renewed for a period of five years from 1 August 2001.

The Registrar's total remuneration is determined by DCMS. It consisted of a basic salary of £56,464 plus a non-consolidated bonus of £6,578 (2003-2004 total emoluments were made up of £54,819 basic salary plus a non-consolidated bonus of £3,100).

	Age	Salary (including Performance Pay)	Real increase in Pension at age 60	Total accrued pension at age 60 at 31.3.05
Dr James Parker	52	63,042	834 (768 in 2003-04)	9,491 (8,657 in 2003-2004)

NOTE 3   GOVERNMENT GRANT RESERVE

All capital expenditure (£11,361 in 2004-2005) is financed from HM Governmet Grant. The Grant apportioned is treated in the accounts as a deferred credit. A proportion is transferred annually to the Income and Expenditure Account over the estimated useful life of the assets as Other Income to cover Depreciation.

	2004-05	2003-04
	£	£
Balance Brought Forward	18,241	42,556
Apportioned from HM Government Grant	11,361	-
	29,602	42,556
Transferred to Income & Expenditure Account	(18,531)	(24,315)
Balance Carried Forward	11,071	18,241

NOTE 4   OTHER OPERATING INCOME

	2004-05 £	2003-04 £
Transfer from Government Grant Reserve	18,531	24,315
Reserve (see Note 12)	-	5,000
Other	144	188
	18,675	29,503

NOTE 5   STAFF COSTS

	2004-05 £	2003-04 £
Salaries	307,928	314,374
Employer's National Insurance	22,896	22,411
Superannuation	42,059	40,690
Redundancy Costs	87,595	-
	460,478	377,475

5(i)   Average weekly number of full time staff employed
        in the year was   15

5(ii)   Employees receiving remuneration over £50,000   0

5(iii) Other than the Registrar, none of the Advisory Committee
        members received any remuneration from PLR.

NOTE 6   TANGIBLE FIXED ASSETS

	PLR Computer	Fixtures, Fittings & Equipment	TOTALS
	£	£	£
Cost			
Cost at 1 April 2004	136,960	63,422	200,382
Additions at Cost	9,542	1,819	11,361
Disposals	(76,123)	-	(76,123)
Cost at 31 March 2005	70,379	65,241	135,620
Depreciation			
Depreciation at 1 April 2004	125,598	56,543	182,141
Charge for 2004-05	14,546	3,985	18,531
Less Charge on Disposals	(76,123)	-	(76,123)
Depreciation at 31 March 2005	64,021	60,528	124,549
Net Book Value at 1 April 2004	11,362	6,879	18,241
Net Book Value at 31 March 2005	6,358	4,713	11,071

The financial effect of revaluing the fixed assets was considered to be immaterial and therefore they have been disclosed at their historic cost value.

NOTE 7   OTHER OPERATING CHARGES

	2004-05	2003-04
	£	£
Administration	181,321	156,430
Accommodation	114,535	84,588
Computer Operating Costs	42,674	39,176
Local Authorities	31,327	37,742
Consultants	23,614	55,353
	393,471	373,289

NOTE 8   OPERATING DEFICIT

	Notes	2004-05 £	2003-04 £
The Operating Surplus of is stated after charging		1,257	84,003
Auditor's remuneration - Audit Fee		17,625	14,000
Operating Leases -	15		
Premises Rental		68,391	39,071
Computer Licences		-	22,587
Travel, Subsistence & Hospitality		24,031	18,574

NOTE 9   PENSION ACCOUNT

This comprises widow's contributions of 1.5% of gross monthly salary deducted from the Registrar's salary.

NOTE 10   DEBTORS

	2004-05 £	2003-04 £
Rent	23,371	16,154
Sundry	1,587	1,409
	24,958	17,563

NOTE 11   **CREDITORS:- AMOUNTS FALLING DUE WITHIN ONE YEAR**

	2004-05	2003-04
	£	£
Sundry Creditors	47,195	32,731
Corporation Tax	1,121	1,700
Public Lending Right - Unclaimed & Undistributed:		
98/99	-	4,643
(189 authors) 99/00	4,229	4,325
(240 authors) 00/01	7,207	8,510
(247 authors) 01/02	7,416	9,591
(422 authors) 02/03	14,971	21,180
(450 authors) 03/04	19,386	40,761
(599 authors) 04/05	38,600	-
	140,125	123,441

NOTE 12   **PUBLIC LENDING RIGHT RESERVE**

	Balance b/f 1.4.04	Transferred from Creditors: PLR Renounced, Returned or Undistributed after 6 years	Public Lending Right Paid	Charge to Income and Expenditure Account	Balance c/f 31.3.05
	£	£	£	£	£
PLR Reserve (a)	7,760	4,733	2,885	-	9,608

(a)   The Public Lending Right Reserve is to cover probable further claims for payment of PLR. This is a statutory right enforceable by law - authors have the right to demand payment from the Registrar. Amounts held as creditors and subsequently renounced by authors, or unclaimed and undistributed after six years are transferred to the Reserve. If this is insufficient to meet claims in the year, an appropriation is made from the Income and Expenditure Account. Under the arrangements of the Scheme any unclaimed payments due will lapse after six years. Such amounts are retained in the Reserve for the benefit of authors. The Registrar considers that the Reserve carried forward is sufficient to meet probable claims.

NOTE 13   RECONCILIATION OF OPERATING SURPLUS / DEFICIT TO NET CASH OUTFLOW FROM OPERATING ACTIVITIES

	2004-05	2003-04
	£	£
Operating Surplus	1,257	84,003
Depreciation charge	18,531	24,315
Release from Government Grant Reserve	(18,531)	(24,315)
Decrease/(Increase) in debtors	(7,310)	3,019,960
(Decrease)/Increase in creditors	17,263	(3,124,877)
(Decrease) in PLR Reserve	1,848	(1,583)
Net Cash Inflow/(Outflow) from Operating Activities	13,058	(22,497)

NOTE 14   ANALYSIS OF CHANGES IN NET FUNDS

	Year ending 31 March 2005	Year ending 31 March 2004
	£	£
Balance at 1 April 2004 and 1 April 2003	118,347	129,439
Net Cash Inflow/(Outflow)	29,461	11,092
Balance at 31 March 2005 and 31 March 2004	147,808	118,347

Net funds comprise only cash at bank and in hand.
There are no bank overdrafts or short-term investments.

NOTE 15   OPERATING LEASES

At 31 March 2005 the Public Lending Right had annual commitments under non-cancellable Operating Leases as set out below.

	2004-05	2003-04
	£	£
Operating Leases expiring within:		
One Year	-	22,587
In the Second to Fifth Years Inclusive		-
Over Five Years	73,044	55,225
	73,044	77,812

106

NOTE 16   CAPITAL COMMITMENTS

At 31 March 2005 there were no capital commitments contracted for, or capital commitments approved but not contracted for (£nil at 31 March 2004).

NOTE 17   NOTIONAL COSTS

Notional cost of capital is calculated as 3.5% of average net assets/liabilities for the year and amounts to £772 (2003-2004 £617).

NOTE 18   RELATED PARTY TRANSACTIONS

Public Lending Right is a Non-Departmental Public Body (NDPB) sponsored by the Department for Culture, Media and Sport. The DCMS is regarded as a related party. During the year PLR has had various transactions with other Government Departments and public sector bodies which can be summarised as follows:

British Library - provision of bibliographic data

Local authorities - provision of loan sample

None of the members of PLR's Advisory Committee, key managerial staff or other related parties has undertaken any material transactions with PLR during the year.

NOTE 19   PERFORMANCE INDICATORS

The key performance indicator set by DCMS is to manage PLR efficiently, cost-effectively and in line with statutory and audit requirements, so as to maximise payments made to authors from the Central Fund; at the same time to support DCMS in the achievement of its overall aims for the cultural sector by prioritising those areas of PLR activity most relevant to the following DCMS objectives:

	Target	Actual
Objective 1	6,556,000	6,536,539
Objective 2	21,890	23,761
Objective 3	894,610	912,200

DCMS Objective 1: Reflects the support provided by the PLR payments to authors to sustain their creativity and livelihoods, thus improving their opportunities to achieve literary success and helping to develop the cultural sector as a whole;
DCMS Objective 2 : Reflects the costs of the Registrar's international development work in support of DCMS's objective to promote abroad the UK's expertise in cultural activities;
DCMS Objective 3 : Reflects the costs incurred by the Registrar and his team in administering the PLR Scheme.

NOTE 20   PENSIONS

The Government Actuaries Department valued the Registrar's pension liability. As at 31 March 2005, the value of pension liability of the Registrar's scheme was £179,633. GAD assumed a discount rate net of price increases of 3.5% per annum in calculating the pension liability (see Note 2).

The PCSPS is an unfunded multi-employer defined benefit scheme but Public Lending Right is unable to identify its share of the underlying assets and liabilities. A full actuarial valuation was carried out at 31 March 1999. Details can be found in the resource accounts of the Cabinet office; Civil Superannuation (www.civilservice-pensions.gov.uk).

For 2004-05, employers' contributions of £42,059 were payable to the PCSPS (2003-04 £40,690) at one of four rates in the range 12 to 18.5 per cent of pensionable pay, based on salary bands. Rates will remain the same for the next two years, subject to revalorisation of the salary bands. Employer contributions are to be reviewed every four years following a full scheme valuation by the Government Actuary. The contribution rates reflect benefits as they are accrued, not when the costs are actually incurred, and reflect past experience of the scheme.

NOTE 21   FINANCIAL INSTRUMENTS

FRS 13 Derivatives and other financial instruments, require disclosure of the role which financial instruments have had during the period, in creating or changing the risks that Public Lending Right faces in undertaking its role.

■   Liquidity Risks

Public Lending Right's income is derived primarily from grants provided by the Department for Culture, Media and Sport. In 2004-2005, there have been no borrowings, therefore it is believed that Public Lending Right is not exposed to significant liquidity risks.

■   Interest Rate Risks

Public Lending Right has no financial liabilities such as bank loans. Cash balances, which are drawn down to pay for operating costs, are held in instant access variable rate bank accounts, which on average carried an interest rate of 3.75% in the year. Public Lending Right consider that the Public Lending Right Central Fund is not exposed to significant interest rate risks.

■   Foreign Currency Risks

Public Lending Right holds cash in a variety of bank accounts (UK and foreign). However, despite the dealings in foreign currency, Public Lending Right believes that they are not exposed to any foreign exchange risks, given the small amounts that are involved.

NOTE 22   CORPORATION TAX

Corporation Tax is due on interest received.

	2004-05	2003-04
	£	£
Interest Receivable	15,199	8,949
Interest Received in Year	15,114	11,025
Corporation Tax @ 23.75% on interest received over £10,000 (19% in 2003/04)	1,121	1,700

The 2003-04 tax figure of £1,700 was not due to the Inland Revenue. We also received a refund of £442 for the year 2002-03. The total tax due is calculated as follows:

Year	£
2002-03	(442)
2003-04	(1,700)
2004-05	1,121
	(1,021)

Printed in the UK for The Stationery Office Limited
on behalf of the Controller of Her Majesty's Stationery Office
ID,180621 07/05

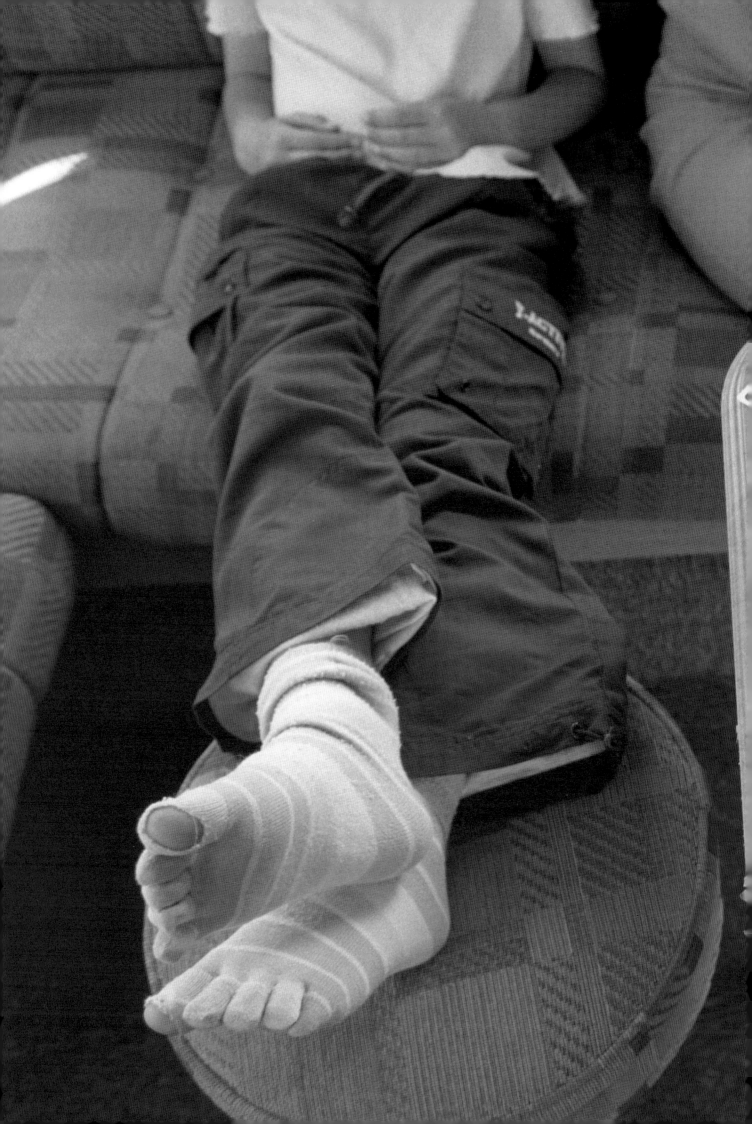